Printed in Great Britain
by Amazon

80021621R00066